PRESENT

PRESENT

ALFRED CORN

COUNTERPOINT

WASHINGTON, D.C.

Acknowledgments are listed on page 101.

Library of Congress Cataloging-in-Publication Data
Corn, Alfred, 1943–
Present / Alfred Corn.
1. Corn, Alfred, 1943–   . I. Title.
PS3553.O655P74   1997
811'.54—dc21   96-51671
ISBN 1-887178-31-7 (clothbound) (alk. paper)

Book design by Cynthia Krupat
Typesetting by Wilsted & Taylor

FIRST PRINTING
Printed in the United States of America on acid-free paper that meets
the American National Standards Institute Z39-48 Standard

COUNTERPOINT
P.O. Box 65793
Washington, D.C. 20035-5793

Distributed by Publishers Group West

for Chris

Contents

I

II

III

Choreography

I

The Shouters

A fiercer form of homelessness, an exile
From the brisk release that conversation offers:
You've heard them on the street, snapped to alert
As they barked cusswords at—what? some blood-red
Ghost that loomed and stalked as you approached.

That sweeping hand, as though it held a gavel,
Flung down a tattered gauntlet or was aiming
Karate chops at an invisible
Assailant, adds the punch of blunt conviction
To words that pump white steam into the cold.

Common explanations, whether hormonal
Failure (aging women diagnostic
Victims of that), schizophrenia, booze,
Downtown attitude or bigotry,
Don't quite account for voices raw as theirs.

What makes you stop and see this one as crowned
With a halo of syringes, each injecting
Various doses of addictive damage
Since childhood, when a parent screamed "Shut up,"
Or the year love crashed down around his head, or—

"Shut *up!*" he shouts (as others have) and shudders
Enough to block overtures always worth
Risking . . . unless it's clear a mind divided
Is getting back at itself and will go on
To heights where the air burns thin and it can shout
And shout until encroaching silence falls—
Sheltered up there, where all our cries are heard.

Stepson Elegy

Virginia Whitaker MacMillan Corn, 1924–1992

Plots of field in piecework, Georgia as quilt, the quilter
Gifted even if slim means restrained her color
Range—gray and tan quickening to green and darker
Green, a miles-long jagged seam of metal river
Slashing the pattern, intersecting at sharp angles
Highway and secondary roads in crisscross suture
That bend around maternal contours of the hills.

Close to the maximum exposure,
A quarter hour of morning radiance
Burning through an airplane porthole
Still hasn't dislodged the ache stuck
In my throat these past two days, days
Of hours spent with old snapshots and recent
Letters I read through a wavering
Liquid pane that didn't quite make
Illegible sentences such as
My family is like a melody, an old
Favorite song gilded with memories,
Dearer to me each time I hear it.

Conditioned by the ban on sentimentality
(For which no moving definition exists)
I couldn't hear that old favorite; and gilt-edged
Memories were interleaved for me with others
Pointless or too dire to dwell on now—
Even though, pulling down the shade, eyes closed,
Yesterday I saw you mysteriously there,
In a dress from back when and the hairstyle
You had before the—what's the term, the treatments,
And the sibylline turban you took to wearing. Yes,
There was the smile that proved you were you, cheerful,
Obviously, because in the new, good, white-columned place

Were no hospitals, mastectomies, or relapses,
No lymphoma, chemo, or IV morphine. Also no pain,
Except perhaps a kind of pale blue mourning for us here
And what you knew we'd day by day be asked to undergo.

———

Funerals, for one thing. Like dying, they've become
An art, and it's too late to curb the ambition
That chose pink satin upholstery, a nightgown
With white lace trim, thick makeup, a left hand
Light as rose petals placed over your heart.
At what point in history did people decide
They should always try to make a "statement"?
From Southern California your New Age nephew
Sent some doggerel to be read, which fear of sounding
Like has kept me from beginning this, like,
For six months and longer. And why not still?
Unspoken promises are hard to break. One month
Before you died, I sent a letter *not* designed
To be thrust at the dozen friends you dragooned,
Who "just loved" that first attempt to sum up
What you'd meant to us. Risk of sounding final
Safely run, I accepted thanks at face value,
And for what was being asked—explicitly? No,
But then we'd been reading each other for years.
Though your own "poetry" was never written down,
You'd seen how private, even trivial events,
Put in a form that balanced feeling with fact,
Might compose a record worth hearing more than once.
Could I do something like that for you? Well, maybe—
Though without the Mantovani strings you'd probably
Prefer, instead, in that uneasy listening
Poulenc–and–Billie Holiday idiom worked out
During the past two decades, the one I could
Recognize myself in. "God Bless the Child" indeed:
For, however solemn our human occasions, the music
Industry's never unselfish enough, right, there
Must always be something in the project for *it*.

In the mid-eighties, you planted a Cherokee rose
(Georgia State flower) in the roomy back yard,
And said so in your special tone, the exact import
This time beyond me. True, I had nothing against
Georgia, wild white roses, or the Cherokee nation,
On the contrary, and, each visit home, as the vines
Climbed or flowered, sang praises (least homage due
Metaphoric shrines crucial to those we love).
This afternoon, aware that house and grounds will soon
Belong to someone who's never even heard of you,
And to take a breather from the gathered mourners,
I've stepped outside and wandered over to the fence
Where it hangs, green sinews stretched right and left
Of the central stock. Or not so green: a blight,
Unnameable as fatal, has struck, with yellow
Leaves and bare, thorned vines left to ruin
A pretty memory . . . Our next-to-last
Heart-to-heart you said you couldn't *taste* anything,
A glass of Sprite was just the same as soda water . . .
Which reminded me how, my first year away at school,
You installed a pop machine in the shop, kept it
Stocked and working, then sent me weekly proceeds,
Handily spent on snacks or movies till time
To get back to the *Aeneid* or some such epic.
The trivia, the nickel-and-dime of memory
Is hardest to accept, burning a hole
In decorum's pocket . . . but if I try instead
To imagine you in a hospital bed, sipping your Sprite—
Your soda water—it's not a turban but a crown
You're wearing (see, I too have lost all sense of taste)
And not of white roses but of plaited thorns.

What saved you, how did you manage to survive
When your pilot husband was killed in a bombing raid
Back in the Second World War's dim antiquity?
Or adjust to remarriage with a handsome if

6

Short-tempered widower, father of three children;
And then attempt to have two of your own,
Both dying in infancy, a misfortune you never
Mentioned without fighting back tears. If only
Poems *were* fiction and those griefs lighter . . .
Considering the bare facts of your abridged
Biography, the double handicap of work
And housework in our poorly sited little house,
Nothing I can say will weigh in the balance,
Nothing sugar over the underlying mourning
You lived in, but never allowed yourself to dwell on
Since, after all, there were so many things
You enjoyed—us, apparently, the familiar
Melody that came at a cost you'd consider
Unchristian ever to mention. There was always
More to do, an extra quilt brought to one
Of our rooms when December winds turned cold,
A passage in First Corinthians read aloud,
Or Easter outfits found for your children,
Like those we still wear in color photos
From an album dated 1952. Also,
A few serene Old Fashioneds to concoct,
Which you and Daddy would share of an evening—
Until he died and left you to consume alone
Your one indulgence in the face of other
Treatments whose pain and indignity
You routinely made light of. This New Age of ours,
What we won't go through in order to continue
Hearing our old favorite songs, gilded
With memories, dearer—but look, I've begun
To copy you, as though I didn't know better
Than to sound too pious or love too much, as you did
Until the end. The end, the end: for, when you go,
So does it all, a whole childhood, a whole fugitive
State, become as ancient and unreal as Troy
Or the"Trail of Tears."

          Now that you've read everything,
I can mention that passage where Virgil, *Il Mantovano,*

Has his hero tell the Sibyl not to write
On leaves lest winds make nonsense of her songs.
To Phoebus and Trivia, Goddess of crossroads,
He promised a shrine: this later Georgian one
Is raised to you and to the Savior, whom
A child now asks to bless, and find a site for
Its Corinthian columns, twined with the Cherokee rose.

Lago di Como: *The Cypresses*

Cupressus lusitanica,
The species name, and factual
Probes in an old *Britannica*
Confirm it came from Portugal.

Greeks, too, arrived as immigrants
And planted the olive at its side,
A Mediterranean romance
Green long after Greek had died.

The drawback? Immobility,
But isn't the breezes' clear intention
To set the rooted captives free
With four fresh knots of intervention?—

Which bends them in a flexible arc
As buried souls wake up again,
Fresh conscripts drawn out of the dark.
Tall, tapering, and midnight green,

They stand as cypress did for them,
Anonymous memorials
Disburdened of the flat pro tem,
In soil thought through by human skulls.

When the trees stir and tremble (much
As their Lisbon cousins might have done
In the great earthquake), only a Dutch
Painter would try to render one.

I'm satisfied to watch as light
Begins to slant and breezes fall.
In shade as dark as minor night,
They hear my tentative footfall,

And breathe a welcome neither Greek
Nor Portuguese, a country drawl,
Seasoned without being antique:
"Come join these ranks for the long haul!

Of course there is an alternative
Less obstinate than our endeavor,
Which only suits those who can give
Notice to time and change forever."

In the distance I see a small van go
Speeding away with passengers,
Who might say "We're not ready," though
What happens happens when *it* prefers.

Becalmed a moment, the trees will soon
Return to their colloquium,
Branches billowing toward the moon
Risen over Elysium.

A Goya Reproduction

In the South Georgia town where I grew up, anyone who wanted to see paintings had to go somewhere else. Apart from a few grinning, humdrum portraits commissioned by this or that moderately well-heeled family, there were none at all. Or almost none: in our very own house hung an oil copy of Landseer's *The Monarch of the Glen*, made by my mother before she died. This magisterial head of an eight-point stag against a background of snowcapped mountains and dark green fir trees was used in magazine advertisements by one of the life-insurance companies—a reproduction that must have been the source of her copy since she can't ever have seen the original. Distance from truth, here as elsewhere, recalls Plato's notorious indictment of poetry—as an imperfect copy of an imperfect copy. My mother's painting took things one step further. It just now occurs to me that she probably associated the stag's regal head with my father, who worked during Depression years for an insurance company, his law degree only one among many things unfitting him for the job. People said he looked like Clark Gable, and certainly he had the self-confidence to match (honed during how many "stag" smokers), which didn't mean he particularly liked taking orders from higher-ups.

The lead-white highlight on the stag's black nose gave it the same moist, rubbery quality as our pet terrier's, with the effect of making the picture less intimidating. My little room at the rear of our house had only two ornaments, *The Monarch* and another oil of my mother's own invention, a panorama that featured on one hand a plump Dutch windmill and on the other someone's not-so-Dutch gondola being poled along Amsterdam's or Venice's placid canals by a boatman in Italianate costume. An artist could slavishly copy, then, or freely invent without realism's dull constraints: Were there other choices? Those mornings when sunlight woke me early, I'd sometimes lie under the bedcovers and stare at the paintings, trying to have thoughts about the person who had done them even though I possessed no actual memories of her. She had died on my second birthday; and I've often wondered whether presents were nevertheless given to me that day or withheld until later. Knowledge of her was always confined to what I had been told by others: that she had been a *good* person, very *pretty,* and that she loved me *very much.* Much later, my father let drop the fact that *her* mother, Zola Johns, was Jewish, though she had married a gentile, Mr. Lahey, an immigrant from Liverpool; but that my mother had been brought up as a member of the Disciples of Christ church, a Presbyterian offshoot. Whether religion was important to her or simply a part of the social life of her place and time, I don't know.

As well as being an amateur painter, she was said to be a poetry lover, which would explain the presence of a worn pastel volume of Keats's poems on our shelves. Nor was the art of music left out: she also played the violin. At some point, around age eight or nine, I found her instrument tucked away in a dusty storage room. Opening the heavy black case brought with it a prickly feeling of violation, which didn't, however, stop me. You'd have had to know more than I did about music and music making not to be frightened by that exotic, sherry-colored piece of cabinetry, its catgut strings broken, the bridge flopping helplessly about. I remember running my finger around the hardwood volutes of the fiddlehead, so like a snail shell or the namesake uncurling sprout of a fern. Mysterious, the function of the symmetrically paired f's cut into the front of the instrument, but at least they offered convenient peepholes into the dim interior: oh, filled with darkness only. I held the violin in the crook of my arm for a while (like a baby?), then replaced it, broken strings and all, in the dusty, velvet-lined case before closing the heavy lid and snapping the lock into place, which clicked shut as smartly as one of Keats's poems, say, the sonnet "To Sleep."

I didn't paint or play an instrument, but I did read. Most Saturdays included a trip to our local Carnegie library, a snug sanctuary built of brick and marble. A dreaded obstacle was the phalanx of bullies often waiting on the lawn outside to pounce on the skinny little weirdo who didn't like to trade punches with them, which would have been the only path to equality and friendship. My humiliating response to being pushed to the ground and pummeled was merely to lie still until the attackers got bored and left. After which I'd get up, adjust myself, and trudge onward. During one of these library visits I came across a book of reproductions of works in the Metropolitan Museum. The book had been assembled for children, its cover a reproduction of Goya's *Don Manuel Osorio Manrique de Zuñiga*. Not the real thing, but accurate enough to capture the attention of someone who'd never seen a great painting—in fact, to form the basis for a devotion to painting no less ardent today. The portrait's attractions for me then weren't formal or painterly, not at the conscious level. I wanted to *be* that little boy. His pomegranate-red suit with its gauze collar and white silk sash, his beribboned shoes, his pet bird and birdcage, the attendant cats—calico, gray-striped, and black— everything seemed to bespeak a world of playful ease with one adored child at its center. I knew that the painter was Spanish, but nothing else about him. He painted, which meant he resembled my mother to at least that degree. Circumstances provided him with subjects like little princes instead of magazine ads, yet if he and she had ever looked each other in the eye a spark of recognition would no doubt have leapt between them.

My own surroundings were anything but princely. Family fortunes had declined beginning with the Depression, and my father, who never fully recovered from the death of my mother just at the end of the war, had settled for the unenergetic expedient of working for my grandfather, with whom he fought almost every day. A large pie wedge of his salary went for Old Grand-Dad whisky. I have a clear visual memory of the butterscotch-colored label printed with a white and gray marble bust of an old man whose benign smile in no way resembled my grandfather's well-meaning but scary rictus. Drink, along with movies and hours-long Sunday drives in his sea green Lincoln, was my father's only entertainment. Can he really have been unaware that the three children in the back seat of that car were practically crazed with boredom as he discharged the parental duty of "spending time with the kids"? Within minutes of the city limits, any highway taken led you through wildernesses not much changed since the days of Ponce de León and later Spanish explorers, who, on forays up from Hispaniola or Cuba, called this semitropical Eden-with-mosquitoes Guale, an approximation of its Indian name. The flat, pine-choked South Georgia landscape, relieved only by an occasional cypress swamp and the splayed fans of palmettos, held no interest for children besotted with movies and comic books.

Yet that same landscape today, despite its limited painterly appeal, has the power to stir up feeling for me as none of the much more beautiful ones that came later. To recall it is also to recall a scent, the pervasive smell of burning pinewood that came from gray, unpainted shacks with no other form of heating than soot-black iron stoves. Here descendants of slaves or white tenant farmers lived, in small frame structures set up on high brick pilings not far from the highway. Porch furniture often included a refrigerator there was no room for inside. Recalling comments on those houses made by grownups expressing compassion and condescension in about equal measure, I think I was supposed to appreciate how lucky we were not to have to live *there.* I did, but the truth is that children are capable of being disturbed by sharp contrasts between wealth and poverty, even if they don't understand why some are rich and some not.

Daddy's Lincoln was eventually traded in for a less expensive car as his means shrank further. My stepmother, who became my second mother when I was five, accepted circumstances more and more subject to the pinch of enforced thrift with a certain shrugging equanimity. Her own father drank, and she wasn't as shocked as I was, those days when Daddy was too "sick" to go in and oversee my grandfather's shop. Eventually she went to work as well, and my older sisters and I learned to take care of ourselves. I didn't know then that there's nothing shameful in being unmoneyed, probably because no one else around seemed to know, either. Never without a red scald of embarrassment did I look, really look, at our drab little white-painted house. The same for my room in it—a sort of utility adjunct at the back door, which had to be turned into makeshift quarters for me when my growing sisters' need for privacy required the removal of any male (however young) from their own private sanctuary. Margaret was two years older, Zoe fully eight years. I was the "baby," and a boy, "sweet" no doubt, but a drag on their own more grown-up activities. It was just as well that I spent a lot of time alone in my room reading.

Beyond the reach of the already overextended oil furnace, that utility room could be glacial in winter. I remember many nights of interrupted sleep, it was so cold. My body curled up in a fetal ball as I thought about all sorts of things: for example, Christmas and what presents I might have a chance of getting, or just strange, half-focused imaginings flickering like foxfire against the darkness. I sometimes counted sheep, but these could easily metamorphose into other animals: dogs, raccoons (with their little black masks), panthers, deer, cattle, donkeys—a whole Noah's Ark menagerie of the animal kingdom, although not peaceable, since they fought among themselves. Another thing I didn't know back then was how angry I was. Anger wasn't one of the permissible emotions. The adults had enough insoluble problems already without having to negotiate with children who complained or talked back. My stepmother did the best she knew how, and presents at Christmas and on birthdays were meant to stress to us that we were loved, in case we doubted.

The reproductions from the Metropolitan were windows onto altogether different circumstances. They joined the growing number of books read and musical works heard that formed my conception of what *real life* was like. Real life was obviously better than mine, otherwise why would people be so eager to go ahead with it? The world of Art was a lifeline, assuring me that, if not here, then *somewhere* there was a realm where order and excitement, beauty and goodness were the norm. It's fashionable nowadays for people who are the product of higher education, museums, and concert halls to grimace at the word *culture* and to make it plain that they prefer something less etiolated. Granted, the *word* won't do, given the uses it has been put to, but I've never myself been able to get over that loyalty to music, art, and literature first formed in childhood. Art worked better than the magician's box of tricks I got one Christmas, whose scarves and coins required hands less clumsy than mine if miracles were going to be performed. Without books, pictures, and music there would have been nothing to draw me on with hopeful anticipation into the brawl, the ice storm that life often is.

I have the fantasy that much the same was true for Goya, born in the bleak Aragonese village of Fuendetodos (109 souls) of parents with nearly empty pockets and a patent, on the mother's side, of minimum nobility, which convinced the untitled Goya acquiring it by marriage that he ought no longer stoop to anything as ignoble as earning an income. Luck for the boy came when his father eventually gave up those pretensions, though not the honorary *Don* before his name, moved to Saragossa and took up his old trade as a gilder. In Saragossa, Goya was given a little schooling and drawing lessons from the local painting master Luzán. Small commissions in Fuendetodos and Saragossa, a sojourn in Madrid, an Italian journey, return to Madrid and marriage to the sister of his painting master, employment in the form of producing cartoons for the Royal Tapestry Manufacture, his first society portraits—all the rest followed in due course. Goya led one of those artists' lives that mostly turn out well—and because of art alone. Nothing else in his origins promised distinction or success.

Of the obscure illness he suffered in 1792, the illness that left him with no hearing and a tendency toward melancholy forever after, Malraux said: "One of the charming artists of the eighteenth century was expiring." If Goya had in fact died, we would have his church frescoes, cartoons, and society portraits but not the works that make us think of him as the first modern painter. During the late 1780s and early 1790s he completed some of his most winsome portraits— the Osuna family, the Marquesa de Pontejos, the Duke and the Duchess of Alba, quite a field of fair folk. These works show an unmistakable influence from the great age of English portraiture (although known to him probably through mezzotint reproductions only, which were widely available on the Continent in those years). Based on such portraits, his reputation would have been secure and small; but the circumstance of compromised health took him a great distance farther.

In the early 1780s Goya was commissioned by the still new Bank of San Carlos to paint likenesses of its directors. Probably the best of this series is the portrait of the Conde de Altamira, who carefully watched Goya's rise to fame during that decade. In 1788 the Count commissioned a portrait of his four-year-old son, Don Manuel Osorio Manrique de Zuñiga. Goya may have received the commission as a welcome reprieve at the conclusion of what had been a year of torments. For some time he had been writing to his friend Zapater that he was feeling his age (he was forty-two, an advanced age in that day) and counting his wrinkles. Among the annoyances and disappointments of the previous several months was his being passed over for the post of Director of the Division of Painting of the Academy of Fine Arts. Instead it was awarded to someone named Ferro, whom we have heard of only because of this incident. Notable paintings of the year include the tapestry cartoon *The Festival of San Isidro,* and there was also a *Saint Francis of Borgia Exorcising a Demonized Dying Man.* Not fully satisfying, this painting is even so the first to introduce phantasmagoric figures—owllike, simian, canine demons hovering over the afflicted patient—into Goya's repertory of expressive imagery. Finally, late in that year, the progressive Bourbon ruler Charles III died, with nearly everyone recognizing his successor as a lout and a reactionary. The brief Spanish Enlightenment was at an end.

Often as not, portraiture for the later Goya was an indictment, the most famous example his 1799 image of the *Family of Charles IV.* Exception is generally made for children, though, who, from the little Countess of Chinchón to the Osuna children and even to the royal offspring of Charles IV, are always presented as adorable innocents who might have stepped out of *Emile.* Don Manuel probably best epitomizes Goya's admiration for childhood and the childlike spirit. Impossible to look at the picture—the soft pink cheeks, the sad, enormous black-olive eyes, the miniature Latin nose, the small cupid's-bow mouth, the loosely hanging chestnut curls, the hint of a four-year-old's normal shyness just barely held at bay—and not melt. The portrait is one of the great sentimental favorites of all time.

But Goya's intentions here can't be summed up as eighteenth century sentiment. His portrait is an allegory of the doom that innocence faces—as I couldn't have recognized thirty-five years ago, when the portrait looked like a celebration of the security and comfort surrounding a little prince. Goya had lost several children by the time this picture was painted, and his son Francisco (the only one to survive to adulthood) was the same age as Don Manuel. Besides, survival isn't the same as being home free. Goya by age forty-two, after a considerable exposure to the world of professional artists, the court, the military and financial wings of society, already knew more than enough about how the world operates ever to feel easy again, neither for himself nor for any child about to grow up and enter it. Apart from his person and his costume, Don Manuel's identity is caught up in the pet magpie he holds by a string. The magpie had been a favorite pet in Europe since the Middle Ages, and one often sees Renaissance portrayals of the Infant Jesus holding the bird on a string just as in this portrait. The picture would have been completed late in 1788—that is, at the beginning of the Advent season—and Goya, painter of so many church frescoes, would not have failed to respond to his young subject's name. Don Manuel is in essence *Dominus Emanuel,* the Lord who is God With Us and embodies the Platonic truth that each person is a copy, however imperfect, of the divine original.

Don Manuel's outfit was fashionable for the time (you see Charles IV's son, standing between him and Queen Maria Luisa, wearing the same thing, plus royal regalia, in the later group portrait). Whether or not fashion took it into account, the white and red of the boy's costume are the liturgical colors of Incarnation and Passion. The intrinsic connection between these two doctrines is an old Christian theme adumbrated in theology, liturgy, and the church calendar. December 26 is the Feast of Stephen, the first Christian martyr. The feast of the Holy Innocents (the children slain at Herod's order after Jesus' birth) follows two days after. Christianity is the religion of the Child who will one day die (and, in divine form, be resurrected). Don Manuel's stiff upright stance, with hands extended to either side, makes of him a little cross.

The boy's magpie is tethered and the birds to his left are confined in a cage, which, although it has a hook permitting it to be suspended in air, is nevertheless on the ground. Such details help portray Incarnation as imprisonment: the birdlike soul caught and held captive in flesh. The magpie bears in its beak a small square of paper printed with an easel, canvas, and brush, tools of the painter's trade; and Goya has inscribed his name there, reminding us that painting is an incarnational art, where immaterial truth must be embodied in form, in volume, color, texture.

Anything that is material, however, is always under siege. Behind the magpie are three crouching cats, the calico with distended topaz eyes fixed on its natural prey as though ready to pounce at any moment. The striped gray, with its feminine face, glances coquettishly off to one side. Behind these, the third black cat is no more than a dark silhouette with two burning coals staring at the bird. This is a mild, early hint of what will appear later in Goya—*The Madhouse, The Burial of the Sardine, Los Caprichos, Los Disparates, The Disasters of War.* The totality of that work is what we think of as Goya, in all his inordinate access to feeling, his grasp of the Iberian earth and the psychology engendered by it, the high temperature of Spanish blood, whether spilled in a bullfight or at the execution of a revolutionary, all this made to cohabit with Goya's cynicism and his phantasmagoria.

In both the Saint Francis painting and Don Manuel's portrait, evil is situated on the side of the painting that is left hand *for the viewer.* It is our evil; we are the persecutors. Meanwhile an unearthly radiance hovers around the head of the boy, whose innocent gaze accuses us not by any perceptible suspicion of us but precisely by the absence of it. He trusts us; he does not see that the cats, according to their nature, have designs on his pet. I have never been able to discover anything about Don Manuel's life as an adult. Did he become a financier like his father? Was he wounded or killed during the Napoleonic invasion? Did his father's wealth disappear in court intrigue or the upheavals of war? In this painting, Don Manuel doesn't know anything of his future, and much of its meaning depends on the tension between his innocence and the visual reminders of the trials most adults must confront.

It was a natural mistake for me at age ten to see art as portraying an unflawed beauty and felicity that must exist *somewhere*. A reckonable amount of it is just that; but more often the drawbacks of incarnation are art's besetting subject, the spirit in its cage of flesh subject to desire, drunkenness, illness, punches to the gut, failing vigor, and at last a severing from flesh that despite everything always seems to come too soon. "When I was a child, I thought as a child." That naïve blindness was a mistake, yes, but one that fed those years' little flame of warm anticipation (like the candle in my magic set), as tutored seeing and understanding probably wouldn't have. A blindness that saw me through—and what else would have worked for the offspring of a violin and an eight-point stag, a bookish hermit in his unheated cell, waiting for Christmas as though *this* year would actually bring (as previous ones hadn't) the present that made it all bearable, under the sign of love.

Maui: Concerto for Island and Developer

Early riser, victor,
interpreter, conductor,
the sun, pure purpose focused in a pale baton of light,
steps up from the nocturnal pit.
Downbeat! as cymbals latent in a golden wave
crash fortissimo against black rock and give
a magisterial cue to winds
weaving counterpoint among palm fronds
while strings of green lianas play in rife
unison, and drops of water drip from leaf
tip to leaf, the pearled percussion of piano top
notes, pouring it on as the tempo speeds up.

Enter the trumpet call's descending figure
as a 747 lands and eager
couples or solitaries crowd the aisles. But one
whose linen suit matches his understated tan
lets the stampede pass before he disembarks.
Look in those green eyes. Gold fever. It works
overtime in runs of bonded notes, strategic flights,
attracting capital and buying votes
that set big wheels in motion—
it's history's most effective lubrication.
Just ask the cabby promised double fare
if he uses the accelerator. What else is it for?
Later, up on the hotel balcony
among high branches of a flame tree, no
reason those eyes shouldn't play
lightly over the well-framed vista. A waiter will supply
answers to questions put, quite happy to
be swayed by a voice that resonates authority.

———

Earthmovers growling at a low pitch slide
back and forth like trombones in the mud
as wizened banyans are tugged
from their sockets. Clearance for months bogged
down in bureaucratic hooha about
ancestral graves comes through at last when heat
is carefully applied to powers that will
or will not be. A-major chords break through it all,
fanfares of top brass greeting shipments from Taiwan.
Ten thousand yards of concrete flow. A skeleton
of steel confronts a bay where seabirds soar.
Butane flame is simmering vats of tar.

———

The final *presto* ratchets through its paces.
Gin meets tonic at the bash, where spinning slices
of lime and lemon float on pings of pure ebullience,
chitchat and rhinestones twinkling as mogul and free-lance
journalist gauge the potential. No sunset
without its shutterbug, its duo for jet
and publicist, who meets the press outdoors
for a stunning *tutti,* in which trade winds ripple fires
of the torches, surf crashes to the accompaniment
of gull cry, of sonic boom—and a few sounds that can't
be heard, like soft crunchings of bone
as a matter-of-fact vulture consumes the fine
wings and breast of a dead tern scooped up
from a shallow grave in the golf course sand trap.

The Bonfire

Lamar Jenks on Death Row at Sing Sing
drops the letter sent from Florida
stares out high windows through the chain-link screen
to where brick walls
meet the sky and the sun sets
a window opposite on fire   atomic white
the brick begins to burn
and the cell his clothes   the little gold
cross around his neck
and his right hand comes clean
in a glove of flame

At King's Cross someone chortles "Get down
them apples" as early morning
wage-slave crowds de-escalate to the tube
and flames rush up to meet them   burning like rocket
exhaust through their numbers up to the snowy street
meeting outdoor air with a flame cold enough
to incinerate the new-fallen snow

The woman has   outside the clinic in Entebbe
all day   in direct sun
sat holding her number
sweat soaking into the cloth
of her turban   breath
comes in short rasps   someone
in white gave her a cup
of water but no the water is burning
and when she spills it the earth
catches fire and spreads to
the clinic and all are caught up
in the inextinguishable
flashbulb diamond

Quai de Béthune   light deflected from facet
to facet in the chandelier
Vivi de Montreuil drifts forward among
the guests   apéritif dangling
from her hand and takes her place
on a sofa   she puts the glass down before
selecting a cigarette
from the vermeil box on the table
Ghislain bowing forward with a lighter
and the transfiguration begins
black satin changes texture but not
color as fire overtakes it
the salon is a corps of flames   vibrant
rhythmic   roaring at a gallop as
the paneling becomes immaterial
gouts of fire exploding outward into the night
and the river down below sends up sheets of flame

Trains huff out of and into the station   its name
both in characters and Roman letters BEIJING
Li Han pushes a cart up to the door
He is frozen in place
as fire boils out
from the wheels and races across the platform up the columns
erasing whole biographies   characters
and letters rewriting everything
in a contagious metamorphosis

This is Espirito Santo province
a worker lights his torch
and thrusts it into a dry bush   which smolders
and then begins burning   the rumor
spreads to strangler figs wrapped around trunks pushes
up to the canopy where monkeys begin screaming
their fur on fire as they leap
from tree to tree roasting missiles fallen dead
conflagration overtakes a village reaches a delicate
hand down to the post office and the blue
green and gold flag waves briefly
as it goes up in flame and turns to gray crepe

Sudan but he does not know the name
of this village   He and other Dinka were taken
in a raid and forced north   These are of Islam and he would not
give up the Lord so they cut the cord back of his ankles
When pain stops he will be a slave and lame   blood has dried
on the dirt floor   Come Lord come   and here is fire
through a hole in the tent it widens   the sun
burns the tent   desert meets this white burning with heat
and surrenders to the greater fire

On Mischief Night in Detroit someone's painted
death's head crouches over a man
lying on the sidewalk in a heap
clutching a shoe tree in his hand   undisturbed
as gasoline is poured over his clothes
he does wake up for a few seconds oh OH as fire
covers him from head to toe   fire that spreads
to the steps of the library engulfing the stones
in red billows that crackle and roar with laughter
as the streets send up columns of flame and acrid incense

Belfast has its rundown suburbs now
Kevin slips the point
of the syringe into his girlfriend's vein
the needle burns   her blood lights
the bathroom mirror starts showering flame on them
the taps   the shower head begin spurting
the air tingles   dances   thunders
fire pours out the window   floods a parked car
the tank explodes   red orange   a siren cleaves
the night   the sound sings and burns through the ear

Beef cattle amble in from the stockyard
outside Bogotá   the automatic hammer
butts a black-furred forehead and when the blow comes,
flame spews out from the skull and floods the room
like napalm as the air fills with the smell of charred meat
and the blood basin
burns and smokes like a burning well

Father Meeker of St. Anthony's   Pittsburgh
murmurs the Agnus Dei
at eight o'clock Mass   snow of early
January   no one came today
Terry   his acolyte this morning
gazes numb at the elements
smooth red hair   still damp
glows in the candlelight
head bowed   nape exposed
finished
without a thought his hand goes out
wax spills over from the candle   then fire
the table burns   a fiery furnace
and both are caught up in it writhing

Overhead fluorescent lights in the lab
on Nekrasov Street hum while
Yelena Milenkova completes the experiment
on particle motion   confirmation is automatic
results beaming onto the screen   the formula
accurately accounts for all data
and when a query appears and she presses
ENTER the screen goes white
in a nanosecond the lab reaches a thousand
centigrade   pictures from the satellite
show a brilliant white light at Minsk

White lights everywhere   widening
begin to merge   grass   trees   asphalt   concrete
alight   Dresden   Toledo   Mogadishu   bright torches
Osaka   Montreal   Petra   Auckland   Pyongyang
the violins   horns   printing presses   *Principia
Mathematica*   on fire   "Nighthawks"   *Glas*
Ajanta   *To the Lighthouse*   Benin ivory
Siegfried   Karnak   The Hall of Memory
fuel for the flame
eternal flame   the substance of language molten
a spontaneous revulsion from hegemony awkward
construction   site   lines   of glass

dismissed   seeing them   in the opera
shun   attention   span   shortening
do we have clearance from the terminal
do we serve
a terminal flame
term   fla

Sugar Cane

Some view our sable race with scornful eye,
"Their color is a diabolic dye."
Remember, Christians, Negroes, black as Cain,
May be refined, and join the angelic train.

PHILLIS WHEATLEY, *"On Being Brought from Africa to America"*

The mother bending over a baby named Shug
chuckles, "Gimme some sugar," just to preface
a flurry of kisses sweet as sugar cane.
Later, when she stirs a spoonful of Domino
into her coffee, who's to tell the story
how a ten-foot-tall reed from the Old World,
on being brought to the New, was raised and cropped
so cooks could sweeten whatever tasted bitter?
Or how grade-A granulated began as a thick
black syrup boiled for hours in an iron vat
until it was refined to pure, white crystal.

When I was a child whose payoff for obeying
orders was red-and-white-striped candy canes,
I knew that sugar was love.
The first time someone called me "sweetheart,"
I knew sugar was love.
And when I tasted my slice of the wedding cake,
iced white and washed down with sweet champagne,
don't you know sugar was love.

One day Evelina who worked for us
showed up with her son Bubba and laughed,
"Now y'all can play together." He had a sweet
nature, but even so we raised a little Cain,
and Daddy told her not to bring him back.
He thought I'd begun to sound like colored people.
She smiled, dropped her eyes, kept working.
And kept putting on weight. She later died of stroke.
Daddy developed diabetes by age fifty-five,

insulin burned what his blood couldn't handle.
Chronic depressions I have, a nutritionist
gently termed "the sugar blues," but damned
if any lyrics come out of them, baby.

Black-and-white negatives from a picture
history of the sugar trade develop
in my dreams, a dozen able-bodied slaves
hacking forward through a field of cane.
Sweat trickles down from forehead into eye
as they sheave up stalks and cart them to the mill
where grinding iron rollers will express a thin
sucrose solution that, when not refined,
goes from blackstrap molasses on into rum,
a demon conveniently negotiable for slaves.
The master under the impression he owned
these useful properties naturally never thought
of offering *them* a piece of the wedding cake,
the big white house that bubbling brown sugar built
and paid for, unnaturally processed by Domino.

Phillis Wheatley said the sweet Christ was brought
here from Asia Minor to redeem an African child
and maybe her master's soul as well. She wrote
as she lived, a model of refinement, yes,
but black as Abel racing through the canebrake,
demon bloodhounds baying in pursuit,
until at last his brother caught him,
expressed his rage, and rode back home to dinner.
Tell it to Fats Domino, to those who live
on Sugar Hill, tell it to unsuspecting Shug
as soon as she is old enough to hear it.

One day Evelina's son waved goodbye
and climbed on board a northbound train,
black angels guiding him invisibly.
In class he quoted a sentence from Jean Toomer:
"Time and space have no meaning in a canefield."

My father died last fall at eighty-one.
Love's bitter, child, as often as it's sweet.
Mm-mm, I sure do have the blues today:
Baby, will you give me some sugar?

The Cloak of Invisibility

Resisting it at first, I wondered why
Luck had elected to single me out
When subjects more deserving went about
Their business in full visibility.

I favored learning, though, and inch by inch
Sank into knowledge like a nodding sleeper
As the windfall of velvet license deepened.
Not even close-ups made the others flinch—

They shrugged off tingles of warm breath on cheek
Or hand as will-o-the-wisps the dark attracts
And made me privy to whatever facts
Devolve on those whose methods are oblique.

Contagion of invisibility!
Objects caught in the mirror's silver grip,
If I so much as touched them, gave it the slip,
Swept into interstellar darkness, free—

Brocaded screen or acned face, lone mountain
Cabin, oil slick, paperbound Spinoza,
All took shelter under the cloak's *sub rosa*
And drowned appearance in a plunging fountain.

And yet. When the young doctor with downcast eyes
Indicates the gash's stagnant green,
And records a diagnosis of gangrene,
What can't be scraped away, he'll cauterize:

Likewise with me. The morning dawned I saw
Erasure would, eventually, betray
The sunlit chronicle we find our way
By, the book of life, that teaches awe

And heals the blind. . . . It seems an endless age
Since I began that volume's restoration,
Coaxing things back to their first destination,
The daily albinism of the page.

Wonderbread

Loaf after loaf, in several sizes,
and never does it not look fresh,
as though its insides weren't moist
or warm crust not the kind that spices
a room with the plump aroma of toast.

Found on the table; among shadows
next to the kitchen phone; dispatched
FedEx (without return address, though).
Someone, possibly more than one
person, loves me. Well then, who?

Amazing that bread should be so weightless,
down-light when handled, as a me
dying to taste it takes a slice.
Which lasts just long enough to reach
my mouth, but then, at the first bite,

Nothing! Nothing but air, thin air. . . .
Oh. One more loaf of wonderbread,
only a pun for bread, seductive
visually, but you could starve.
Get rid of it, throw it in the river—

Beyond which, grain fields. Future food for the just
and the unjust, those who love, and do not love.

Little Erie Railroad

In the North, in December, a costly Christmas toy
Cleaves a path through drifts of crystallized
Ether, and spruces shaped like spruce cones dot
White hills around the track (elliptical,
Bemused, a forward ladder that never concludes,
Its parallel rails in polished silver
Deftly stapled to fresh redwood sleepers).

Vibrations and a distant fife note signal
The golden locomotive's precise and long
Deferred arrival—which now spins into view
Like a thrown discus, do you see the wheels
Cycling in tandem, dynamic, dynamic, dynamic,
"I *am* here! . . ." But then its streamlines erase themselves,
Banner headline of the high whistle sidling

A half step down in pitch as caboose dwindles
To a crimson spark, fine tingles in the track
Sole proof our fleet forsaker was ever here.
Wait. It has stopped. A spout from the water tank
Dips down to kiss the intake, which swallows
A braid of ice water. Meanwhile puffballs
Of angel hair are huffed aloft from the stack.

There. It's done, the conduit withdrawn, a forward
Jolt, and they're off to the races, with a hoot
Echoing through tunnels swiftly negotiated,
Slung coda of cars in mother-of-pearl and gold
Snaking along behind when it slows for the curve
Then bends into the next straightaway as snow
And evergreens whizz into blurred bands of color.

To locate its motives you'd have to pry open
The fire door, whose hinges give a tiny shriek

Of merriment at spoonfuls of proffered coal,
Each separate lump inscribed with fossil fern.
The furnace within burns bluish white, where flame
Is frozen vapor at absolute zero, converting
Fuels consumed to variable speeds around

The circuit. Miles to go, and the sleepers groan
When its oily golden belly passes over them.
At nightfall, a tiny carbide headlight flicks on,
Projector's beam hurled onward into a moonless *film noir,*
Adding what seems like conjuration to impromptu
Salvos of constellated fireworks—no doubt
Even more touching when viewed from a certain distance.

Parallels

A song of praise runs parallel to fact.
What psalms present is pure experience.

As mirrors praise or blame the facts they show,
So facing mirrors judge themselves alone:

Each, in mirroring mirroring in each,
Reflects contrary counterfeits of truth,

A glass-green emptiness in shrinking frames.
Contempt? It's nothing but reversed self-loathing.

Imagine, instead, an act of conciliation,
Someone recalling how much there was to praise.

Imagine a plain with tracks to the far horizon,
A pair of rails intent on the same point.

Parallel lives. . . . Since everything that rises
must converge, perhaps they're moving upward?

II

HOLY LANDS

The Dead Sea

Inventing a holy land,
who would have settled for these
neutral hills bare except for scrub and sage,
a sky unclouded as impenetrable,
now and then the timeless Bedouin tent—
which would explain, along that ridge,
a straggling flock of goats
with stretched-out, walking shadows?

And now the eastern approaches. Yet nothing
about the frontier's fenced compounds
suggests the traveler en route elsewhere
should stop—even if gunning the engine can't
do much toward canceling those pictures,
the color of pain, a visual undersong. . . .
Once coppergreen expanses of water
slide into view, though, no one could fail
to sense the difference in being
below sea level—air heavy
in the ear, oxygen-rich, cool, dry,
scented with desert, and holy enough.
A hand dipped in water ponders
the viscous feel of minerals in solution,
and little tumuli of salts and carbonates
build a submarine city sprawling
for miles under the hammered-metal surface.
On a shore hazed with distance, neat rows
of date palms identify themselves
with a green herringbone frond and ripen
foodstuffs for, say, the heavenly banquet.
Ritual ablution even so has coated
your skin with a pale silt glove;
and sea and desert are one.

Remember the hands, calloused and sunburned,
of the Qumran scribes, seated at a cave's mouth,
negotiating light that dawn brought back
with the promise of deliverance.
Shadow and light, black fire
on white fire, the unswerving word,
conferring a sacred indifference
to an urban, merely visual appeal.
The caves, dark sockets in a cliff wall,
return no one's gaze today,
even if they once did see
a mountain range of crumpled felt,
cast-iron eagles fixed on invading standards,
and a southbound Jordan feeding the same
fluid body, ever more
mineral, ever heavier with salt.

Jaffa

Tel Jaffa's Mandate-era clock tower
no longer pays much attention
to wavewashed rocks offshore, where travelers
late as the first century rowed out
to inspect the sea monster's ribcage
and rusty remnants of the broken

manacles that helped Andromeda keep
her father's word. Our sunburns sympathize
with the young sacrifice's skin, exposed
to killing UV rays—briefly dimmer
when a fleeting silhouette eclipsed their whitehot
source, and Perseus in wingèd sandals

skated the crest of an upthrust thermal,
Cap of Darkness and Medusa's head
bundled together in his leather pouch.
So Hellenism swept into Asia Minor,
the event commemorated in bleached bones

that had felt it coming as a liquid green
reptilian eye took in his sword's advance,
bronze stabbing downward with the noonday light.
Fetters soon to corrode relaxed, surrendered.
The royal gazette detailed plans for a wedding.

On the *Aladdin*'s stucco terrace, pink
and gold hibiscus framing the seaward view,
we raise a glass. Asked why the tower clock
hands don't move, a mustached waiter adjusts
dark glasses and admits he doesn't know.

41

Caesarea

A theater facing the sea,
Ranked seating like folds
In marble drapery
Or marching Roman legions.

Toppled columns, each drum
An epoch wrapped with the same
Stonecrop. The wild acanthus
Copies a capital

In green, supplying thorns
To a site as reckless as sand
Where visitors late in the day
Erase this morning's footprints.

What audience but ghosts
would still be here, captive
to Medea's rage, or Creon's—
Latin or Greek reverberant

In *personae* with tragic scowls,
Their stance hoisted by buskins
To the plane of pure idea. . . .
Yet a feat of perspective

Lifts the sea still higher:
Above the actors' heads
Waves break, the sun takes its bloodbath,
And a trireme beats shoreward,

Oars tensed aloft and streaming
Salt diamonds into the sea.

In Safed

Joseph Karo was one
who went out from here
dressed in white robes, down
from the city on the hill
to greet the *Shekhinah,*
Presence of *En Sof,*
out in the tilted fields.

Light will
glaze an ivy leaf
fastened to the wall
of the Abu Hav school,
and stone lions face off
over the doorpost of Ha-Ari.
The plain of Galilee
stretches away into afternoon.
When the body dies,
where is Presence then?

On Friday at sunset
lions and ivy leaf
retreat into shadow.
The Sabbath Bride appears:
by lighted candles
words remember the words
that Joseph said.

November–December 1987

Philosophy

Beginning with a fundamental, which
Sounds tonic depths, then reasons up from there,
The will to truth parts company with prayer,
Though both first come to being in a ditch.

Firm axioms advanced and bootstraps tugged
Aloft, it goes as high as we allow
Arguments to pass that don't quite follow,
While strict accounting daydreams as if drugged

On the tough beauty of the whole design,
And heretofore unruly percepts dance
The hidden measure within circumstance,
Mind at the dominant, in pure outline.

———

Nevertheless outside the door, second
Thoughts gather and, when qualified, approach
With mild petitions that no argument
Intent on simple justice can dismiss—
In fact, will find intriguing in themselves,

Fine distinctions that open a zigzag,
Ironic fracture in the system. Meanwhile,
An enharmonic corollary sings
Out, and its modulating emphasis
Makes of doubt a decent countercurrent

Whose keenly passionate analysis
Shows where terms lose their meaning, catapulted
To the chill brink of the inconceivable,
Until thought stops going in that direction,
Direction itself having by then faded. . . .

The tone and tempo of tragedy surface
In a final discourse deep as abnegation:
True love of truth is unrequited love.
High up among towers on the crag of reason
Last fires die down and winter solstice dawns.
Nothing worth proving fails to gain distance

From falsehood by vigilant understatement,
The serious ruin a minor premise survives.
Once distilled, it will find a niche among
Those classic formulae fed to novices,
A bridge to the abbey across which stolid donkeys
Toil, bearing heavy reams of fresh parchment.

Musical Sacrifice

1.

Eisenach, birthplace (in 1685) of J. S. Bach. Close by, on a high hill, Schloss Wartburg, the Thuringian landgraves' ancestral stronghold. Which also sheltered music, judging from Elisabeth's aria in Act II of *Tannhäuser,* a paean addressed to the castle's Great Hall as she waits for the Minnesänger to file in and join her. Music to fortify a fugitive Luther as well, who spent the winter of 1522 there, translating the Bible into dynamic German—and composing hymns. His chorale *Ein' Feste Burg* is most itself when set with strong supporting columns of vertical harmony, like a stone fortress built on some cloudflown crag overseeing the Kingdom. That high hill would also have cast its shadow over the boy Johann shortly after his father's death, which left him an orphan in the care of an exacting older brother.

(Chorale)

Passing through streets both small and broad
To Latin school, he hummed the theme
"A Mighty Fortress Is Our God,"
And stared up toward the snowbound castle.

Mother had died, and, after, Father.
Since Adam's fall we all must die,
Yet death stands warrant of our hope
To reach God's glorious court on high.

2.

Prague, baroque outpost of Austro-Hungary, birthplace (in 1883) of Franz Kafka. *Praha,* the "little mother with sharp claws," whose precincts were topped by a castle—Hapsburg decrees trickling down from it, with consequences for lives being led below in Czech, German, or Yiddish, a populace teeming across cobbled squares, men buttoned into the correct black suit with cravat, a bowler perched on their heads. From Malá Strana to Powder Tower to the Altneu *Shul,* magnetic fields fan out, the stone machine of category and rank in dependable operation.

(Sprechstimme)

Choose an unlikely figure, *Kaffeehausliterat,*
minor functionary, Jew, a glass ceiling
overhead, latest subject in the social laboratory,
which has him threading, like a white rat, baroque
labyrinths of alleys, streets, bridges and stairs
that might or might not lead to air and sunlight,

brilliant prospects over the town, intimacy with,
at decent distance, a Father in his stronghold.
But how to enter? *Das Schloss*: "castle" or "lock,"
His key, nothing more than lunch-hour daydreams. . . .
Two fiancées in succession, intelligent,
sensitive; but not right, not right for him.

From the overlords, genteel racial disdain
but partly concealed. Parents, sisters, whose mere
health was a reproach to his own alienated body.

And writing: serious mistake, indeed, transgression, and yet mandatory. Friends consoled themselves with music: him, though, it overpowered, "like the sea," or a wall around his mind.

"I am chained to invisible literature with invisible chains."

3. *Having Journeyed on Foot to Lübeck to Hear*
Buxtehude, J.S.B. Goes to the Sea and Watches
a Horse and Rider on the Sands

(Toccata)

Crystalline cold, the rocking thunder
Adjunct to sun in galloping triples,
Sand underfoot, a sea to the right,
High waves of brine collecting to fall
In tumbling explosions, coldest of fires.
Will no wave rise without lifting the sun in replica?
O burn, O freeze, O burn!
Frozen starlike in the salt of a gallop,
A rocking thunder over the dunes, head bent
Forward next to the mane as a freezing stream
of diamond wind flames across horse and rider,
Sunburned by cold in a rocking sequence
Thundered back by the crash of a wave
Tipping over in a blue-and-gold gallop,
And must it stop playing its well-tuned welter
Of tangled blue manes, its foam-whitened gold?
O freeze, O burn, O freeze!
Rivered burning in the riptide gold,
Salty evangel declaiming triple thunder
That pounds an anvil of sand, the icy keyboard
Headlong hooves thunder over under the blue.
O burn, O freeze, O burn!
From triune Godhead comes the informing Spirit,
And gives us savor of eternity:
The soul borne upward on a faithful mount
By grace alone will scale high Heaven's ramparts.

4. F.K. at Lugano (1911)

(Waltz)

Where lemon flowers constellate among dark leaves
and sweeten rising updrafts, water colors the view
for grand hotels, the lake staining deeper blue

at twilight to the flat clank of a church bell.
On the esplanade, yesteryear's white-haired string ensemble
dodders through something *echt* Viennese for guests

in boiled shirtfronts or mauve silk, sipping *aperitivi*:
the allure of lowered eyes, her enigmatic smile
borrowed from Mona Lisa, the late season's fatal

Madame X holding in thrall consumptive poet
or firebrand *metteur en scène,* who in her vibrancies
hears soaring Venusbergs or the final Liebestod.

"My dear Felice," F.K. would write a long year later,
"I feel as though I stood outside a locked door
behind which you live, and which never shall be opened."

Still later, after Franz Ferdinand had been shot
and the Great War unleashed, his daydream antidote
was sifting the potpourri of that lost era, when

malaise had infused the psyche only, a fragrant dust
in Europe's neurasthenic *Götterdämmerung,*
the switch thrown on ranks of Edison lightbulbs,

whose moonglow set the stage for a drugged, experimental
waltz with dark specters, ultimate masked ball
of civilization on the eve of a blood cure.

5. 1722: Anna Magdalena's Little Clavier Book

(Allemande)

Among the lessons taught to all below
Are some that bear rehearsal more than once:
"We die, but when death comes we do not know."

My dear Maria died, almost as though
Early departure meant blest deliverance
From painful lessons taught to all below.

Thought of our children constrained to grow
Up orphans, paupers sunk in ignorance,
Could scarcely bear rehearsal more than once.

My early trials, how many years ago,
Were fruit of Father's undue confidence:
We die, but *when* death comes we do not know.

A second wife, then, fair, but not mere show,
Who'd let no child of Bach's turn out a dunce,
Teaching them lessons all must learn below.

Pride had demanded that I should forego
Love's gentle leadings. Gratefulest penance
Be mine to rehearse, then, and more than once.

Anna requested help with clavier, so
I put together a little book (a dance
Suite), and those ornaments she did not know

The fingering of, at last, began to flow.
Etudes, yet wrought and brought to utterance
By hard or tender lessons learned below—
Some of which bear rehearsal more than once:
We die, but when death comes we do not know.

6.

I discovered them both in 1963 and felt even then something reso-
nant in the juxtaposition, two temperaments completely new and yet
somehow familiar. Long, late hours spent replaying the First Bran-
denburg's Adagio, which conveyed better than any music known to
me before what might be called the *mysterium tremendum,* an aura of
sacred fear like a pearl-gray cloud between us and unfathomable de-
ity. Oboe, violin, and basses one after the other state and restate the
gradually descending theme against a shifting ground of sustained
string chords, bass line often the seventh of dominant and
secondary-dominant chords. The effect is of hard-pressed determi-
nation, the soul testing its powers of understanding when confronted
with Creation from the first night until this, the Dorian mode's rug-
ged heft mustered to convey a sense of ineluctable will accomplish-
ing its ends in a world of mute suffering, the human particular left in
the dark as to what upheavals might mean or not mean while being
subsumed under the Mystery. . . . And yet promised by abrupt mod-
ulations into major during the movement's final bars, to keep alive a
sense of expectancy and replenishment. Which the last movement
delivers.

As for reading Kafka, there will never again be a first encounter like
that one, beginning, one cold February night, with *The Trial,* whose
blinding glare didn't let me sleep until I'd raced, stumbling and fall-
ing, to the end. Transparent style and direct reporting of a character's
dilemma activated fiction's deepest resource: identification, the I.D.
in this case a set of papers that, far from constituting Josef K.'s pro-
tection under the law, in advance condemned him (like all out-
siders—racial, cultural, sexual) to a final exclusion. "In the Penal
Colony" came next, a courteous peep into Hell, describing some
imaginary Devil's Island equipped with a machine designed to en-
grave sentences like HONOR THY SUPERIORS and BE JUST on the
bodies of the condemned and self-condemned. And then *The Castle,*

comedy at its most appalling, a pilgrimage, as much workaday as spiritual, through the frozen corridors of bureaucracy, in which red tape comes to resemble ribbons of blood flowing from the spot where administrative slapstick has struck a bit too hard on the petitioner's head, a stupid grin on his face as the Castle once more denies his request for an audience.

7. 1913: F.K. Publishes His First Book

(Scherzo in B-minor)

What, merely because your bumptious friend Brod
insisted you visit busy little Leipzig,
then flung you at *Meineherren* Rowohlt and Wolff;
and merely because those worthies professed to admire
some bleak-spirited trivia you call *Meditations,*

you bowed and let them serve the public *Kafka?*
Brilliant! Wasn't that you reading Heine last June
at your window, a bluebottle fly buzzing and bumbling
around your ears? Fly lit on page, then *bang!*
you snapped shut your book, which then fell open again:

Black goggle eyes and glassy winglets lay flat
around a speck of dark-red blood, in an instant
kaput and dry. Which triggered your brooding, "I am
that fly, who've done myself in." Ah, now the blunder
's been entombed in hard covers, are you content?

Write, if you must, but banish all thoughts of publishing!

8. *1723: Johannes-passion* in Leipzig

(Recitative)

And it came to pass in those days
that the elders of the Council of Leipzig
summoned candidates for the post of Cantor
for St. Thomaskirche in the city,
among them, Johann Sebastian Bach.
The Council did not rule in his favor
but instead invited Telemann, who declined,
and then Graupner, who also declined.
"As the best could not be obtained,
we must take the second-rate."
So concluded the deliberations.

Yet the Council even so demanded
an example of sacred music wherewith
to judge the celebrated organ master;
thus did he compose a Passion
after the gospel that bore his name.
Not yet satisfied, the elders demanded
a letter of dismissal from the Prince,
his previous employer, and having at last
received it, installed the new Cantor
in June of that year of our Lord.

(Arioso)

And are they named St. Thomas Church to doubt
The man He is and works He has done, too?
Almighty God forgive the proud, who flout
Thy commandments, for they know not what they do.

And, Father, grant the strength to keep that head
Unbowed when henchmen come with jeers and flail:
A crown of thorns is well, so He be fed
On that high Love which cannot ever fail.

9. *1917: The Onset*

(Nocturne)

He had done as much as *will* can perform.
Had even moved into a fine apartment
in the Schönborn Palace, where you might live
decently with a new wife among vases of flowers—
as though you had left Prague behind, were less
in the grip of its musty stone fist.

Yet after her summer visit, he couldn't say.
Who stood, who watched, as her train withdrew, a phrase ringing
in his ears: *The alarm trumpets of nothingness?*
Utter oblivion. Early August doldrums sat
deathlike, burning leaves on all the lindens. . . . One day
he spat fresh blood: his lungs' broken vessels had learned to speak.

To lie awake all night, headboard acreak in the heat,
unfinished drafts invisible in the darkness—
though he could, if need be, feel his way and find them.
A thunderstorm launched its bolts at the sleeping city,
quick volleys of unmeaning light, then giant drumrolls,
alarm trumpets of nothingness. . . . With dawn came rain,
gray light sifting through gently stirred curtain lace.

10.

Musikalisches Opfer, with no article, the noun always translated "Offering," though the German more often means "sacrifice," in the sense of sacred ritual. "Musical Sacrifice," then, one exacted by that musical monarch, Frederick II of Prussia, who had appointed Carl Philipp Emanuel Bach his accompanist in 1740. The elder Bach was several times summoned to the Stadtschloss in Potsdam by his royal admirer, always refusing, until excuses courted insolence. So at last in May 1747, he came to his son's house in Potsdam, half blind, weary, dusty from the journey. Word of his arrival reached Frederick at Sans Souci, who sent for him immediately, not even giving him time to change into court dress. The king canceled his customary Sunday evening musicale, and "der alte Bach" was ushered into the royal presence. Everyone has heard the story of Frederick's request: Will you sit at the clavier and improvise a fugue for us?

The composer asked the king to give him a theme and got a chromatic one in C-minor. Bach clasped his wrinkled hands, then took up the gauntlet to produce a three-part ricercare (the older term for a work with fugal texture), apparently delighting his audience. Then Frederick asked him to improvise a fugue with six voices, which Bach politely said he could not do: even mastery has its limits. On returning to Leipzig, however, Bach wrote out from memory the ricercare in three voices, devised another in six voices (responding to the king's challenge) and spun out as well ten more ingenious canons taking various approaches to the theme. One of these, subtitled "Per tonos," modulates up a whole step in pitch each time the canon repeats, rising higher and still higher, as if scaling a mountain. Not often are technical stunts as expressive as this one, and yet it is less ingenious than other sections of the work, which take canonic texture to even higher levels of complexity. Considering the occasion and the labor voluntarily expended, it's clear why Bach might have given the name he did to the work, printed the following autumn with a dedication to Frederick and sent on to Potsdam like a bread-and-butter note.

Musical Sacrifice, like the more highly developed (though never completed) *Art of the Fugue*, is scored for no instruments in particular, a purely theoretical or pedagogical work reminding us that for Bach creation was happily married to instruction. He sought in these various realizations to produce not only a work of art but an exemplum as well of one or more technical features. No peak of formal difficulty was considered too steep to conquer—as long as sight and breath remained.

11. A Sacrifice for Sans Souci

(Canon)

Each year I take a step up the long stairs,
Remembrance flies to youth as to a glade:
The agile keyboard virtuoso tears
Through a fugue no middling fumbler could have played.

Remembrance flies to youth as to a glade
Where will delights in lively conversation
Through a fugue. No middling fumbler could have played
Like that, high ardor at one with calculation.

Where will delights in lively conversation
Take a young man? To marriage, for a start.
Like that high ardor at one with calculation
We have called "music," courtship won her heart.

Take a young man to marriage. For a start,
A child, then two, then more, like steps and stairs.
We have called music "courtship," one her heart
Quickened to hear, at times, quite unawares.

A child, then two, then more, like steps and stairs.
All talented! Whatever music they
Quickened to hear—at times, quite unawares—
I played and taught each one of them to play.

All talented! Whatever music they
May later master, this first shall not rust.
I played and taught each one of them to play
Exactly. Other things the best, I trust,

May later master. This first shall not rust.
Is not fine art, before all else, technique?
Exactly. Other things—the best, I trust—
The soul open to God will surely speak.

Fine art is not, beyond all else, technique.
The agile keyboard virtuoso tears
The soul open to God, who will surely speak
In each resounding step of the long stairs.

12.

Early in *The Castle*, K. attempts to get through to the palace officials by telephone, only to hear a sort of buzzing, "yet not a hum, the echo of voices singing at an infinite distance—blended by sheer impossibility into one high but resonant sound, which vibrated on the ear as if it were trying to penetrate beyond mere hearing." What happens when you associate those high voices with the chorus of Bach's masterworks? Revived by Mendelssohn early in the nineteenth century, the Passions according to Matthew and John eventually became part of standard choral repertory throughout Germany. Wagner knew these consummately theatrical works; nothing easier than for him to consider the anti-Jewish verses of the Passion text in the Gospel of John as adjuncts (along with Luther's anti-Jewish writings) to his own polemic in behalf of unalloyed Germanic genius. Bach's intentions notwithstanding, when audiences heard the call for crucifixion attributed not to "the people," but to "the Jews," a conscious or unconscious connection was established. Supreme art fueling the onrush of historical evil.

F.K.'s escape from the Shoah was accidental: incurable tuberculosis killed him a decade before Hitler's Reich. TB was also the metamorphosis that had been an excuse for breaking his second engagement to Felice. With no wife to care for him, he had to rely on the efforts of his youngest sister Ottla, who took him to her house in the country and tried to nurse him back to health. He regained enough strength to travel to Berlin, where at last he met Dora Diamant, the companion he had been seeking. A brief period of happiness followed, his first and last. In April of 1923 his friend Hugo Bergmann urged him to make literal the Passover promise of final return, a celebration "next year in Jerusalem." He had been studying Hebrew in an effort to recover the Judaic traditions that secular modernism had replaced. Emigration remained a possibility; but that next year, in terrible pain from tubercular throat lesions, he died, leaving *The Castle* incomplete.

Ottla had married a Czech gentile, a legal status that, after Bohemia had been annexed by Germany, provided her with an immunity from deportation. She refused to profit by the loophole, however; fearing that her children would be implicated, she divorced her husband and registered as a Jew. She was first sent to Terezín and then volunteered to accompany a consignment of orphans being shipped to, she believed, Denmark, but in fact to Auschwitz. There, in October 1943, among searchlights, electric fences, and early snow, she died.

13. *Die Verwandlung*

(Symphonic poem)

We are nihilistic thoughts, *kafkas,* jackdaws,
crows in the mind of God,
who, as we do, has bad days—and thought of us
on one of His. Crows hoping to be translated
to Heaven as though unaware Heaven
to be itself requires the absence of crows.
Not to violate those precincts—do you follow, Ottla?—
we must prevent Heaven from thinking of us again.

One afternoon, high up on the Laurenziberg,
our Prague far down below, buildings built
all of smoke, block upon gray block of smoke,
I watched a flock of crows
mount up into the sky in a long line and thought,
Those wings are book bindings, and our books, the steps
of a staircase that breaks off in the sky—
No, rather, a book is a key to the hidden rooms
within the fortress of one's own self,
a black key having the shape of a crow.

I ought to be able to invent words
capable of blowing the odor of corpses in a direction
other than straight into mine and the reader's face.
It was wrong, Ottla, to have allowed those thoughts
to enter your mind—and to bring my illness
to your house, where without the ghost of a complaint
you tried to restore an ailing elder brother
to health again, whether or not he believed you could.
If I could have written myself well again for you!

65

Once, after you had fed us a small supper,
we sat by the hearth at a low fire,
an orange glow wavering among communicating coals.
A sheaf of gold chrysanthemums sat on top of the piano.
The vase replaced one my elbow had knocked over,
inadvertently, a few days before.
I watched you shovel ashes into a bin, and a daydream,
no, some cinematic phantasm overtook me.
A spark from the coals leapt to my mouth and burned
my lips—but burned away as well the pain of burning.
I saw ashes falling from a great height through space,
falling, falling, as though they might never
get to the bottom of things.
And was tempted to look for their source,
some altar or furnace high up that had produced them;
say, vast numbers of crows heaped up together and burned.
What made me turn away from those images?
Who knows, but they were replaced in thought by a music—
frightening, yet one that I, who always avoided music,
didn't choose not to hear. The figure running across
the keyboard was myself, my footfalls
sounding the notes; and others were running,
fleeing from the catastrophe, each foot
landing on a key as, unawares, we all cooperated.
Was it a fugue of death, a human counterpoint
made by fugitives? Composing not the music
we'd have otherwise produced, but what our flight
from death wrung out of us collectively.

A great hand like the shadow of a bird
approached and began removing, in midflight,
each running figure,
so that voices of the fugue, one by one, dropped out.
Until, at length, no more than two of us remained,
who then stopped running. Oh, but
it was you, Ottla, you were the other,
standing there on a white key, and I, on a black one.
Having so much to say meant we could say nothing,
and nothing inhabited the space between us,

66

a nothing that bloomed full and golden.
Then I felt myself being taken up; yet didn't tear
my gaze from yours until its silent music
had been translated into darkness,
all my nothing consenting to be absent from the world.
The Holy of Holies opened and nothing was in it.
You were free, Ottla, your name no longer "Kafka,"
and thus were allowed to live. This is why I fell silent—
do you recall?—that dark afternoon by the fire.

14. *1750: J.S.B. Dictates His Last Work From the Deathbed*

(Chorale Prelude)

When we in greatest need do call
Upon His name, may Jesu send
His strong assistance lest we fall,
And help us make a holy end.

When I in sorest need, in blindness, must
Prepare to bid farewell, my labors done,
The hand that rests upon my brow, I trust
As Love that nothing shall divide me from.

This life has been a prelude and a vale
Where all things teach Thy children Who Thou art.
So may the faithful not forget to hail
Thy cross and glory, Lord, when they depart.

Before Thy throne I shall have trod,
To hear the judgment held in store,
The plea I offer nothing more
Than that Thou diedst for me, O God.

The grace that was and is sufficient guides
Even the lost sheep safely to the fold.
Sing, blessèd choirs of angels as of old:
"Nor Sin nor Death prevails where Love abides!"

Amen, Alleluia, Alleluia, Amen, Amen.

Michel Gérard's Observatory

In the beginning he made it, the grave
weightiness of light,
charcoal's bleak corrosives diagramming his sculpture.
The fleshly character of metal will preserve
tender imperfections created
by hands that never actually touched the work,
the master craftsman who conceived it
toiling, with the cushioned palm and back of his hand,
at an intimate remove.

Like earth's firstborn at the first day's close,
we look at the sky and setting sun
across the surface of an ocean overlaid with fog
as white as arctic snows.
The sun's bald head rides low beside us
above the plain of mist
so as to leave tufts of down
around your temples—just as that divided gaze
tries to encompass both north and south poles
and the thoughts in our two separate languages.

A dragonfly airplane inches across the sky
with the rumble (tame, compared to a spaceship's)
of an engine or a steamer
from the prewar turn of the century.
The days of the black- and redsmith, hammer and sickle,
are gone, as well as the era of Hephaestus's
misshapen appeal. Ours isn't the age of homelessness—no,
instead, of exile, an exile fixed at the line
where sky and earth intersect.
As though launched from two points of origin
separated by incalculable distances,
love found room in a single heart.

We are a new people among other people,
a nation wandering at will over the world,
this, in a day when nomadic cultures are pronounced
defunct in schoolbooks telling old stories
we came to disbelieve: you, in French,
I, in Russian. A people
who must somehow manage without homesickness,
who feel nostalgic not for a place
but for the comfort of being at one
with a time outside mortal limits.

Remember that sensation of not being able
to read either the face or hands of the clock?
And, later, when we *had* learned, how time changed then,
breaking out of the dial, which then dragged us in
like objects, one more cog or wheel or spring,
under its glass cover.
Every moment proved to be measurable,
all the way, we saw, to the end of our lives.
Isn't this why you keep gazing into the face
of constellations spilled out like sand from an hourglass,
hoping that they, at least, are everlasting?

Obeying an invisible rheostat,
our globe darkens,
and the universal planetarium lights up for us.
What dreams it sees, it wills into reality:
the threshold of the twenty-first century,
where we won't spend very many years. We won't,
but the stones will, iron ores now hidden
deep in the earth. Up from those dark mines,
his lantern bright as a full moon, comes the chimney-sweep,
who closes the door after whisking out the stove;
by morning it has cooled down again.

Translated from the Russian of Marina Temkina

The Unknown Poets

1.

Who, glimpsing her crow silhouette
against a lamplit wall that night
of fog and mizzle, would ever know?
A damp trudge home with headcold sniffles,
which had been maddening to stifle
during the long hour while a famous
name recited to a packed house.

The mirror gives her a strange look
so she reopens his new book
and tries to read. It's useless, though.
You'd almost prefer something uncouth.
If asked, she'd turn from the bookshelves
to say, We write of course for ourselves—
and no doubt blush for the half-truth.

2.

The laureate he most admired wrote
back, just once. A world of finesse
in small black script! The other letters
went unanswered—which hurt, but then
it freed him from at least the guilt
that goes with stealing time from writers
who need their hours at the desk.

Bless Dickinson! He told a friend
the story of her handmade booklets.
His own best efforts cried and pled,
so at last he had them printed and bound
at the copier's: one blue, one red,
one black. Felice, after he died,
would read them, once. And when *she* died. . . .

3.

Original but quiet, you didn't
know a soul, no one who read much.
Sometimes perception stood and spoke,
and the ground buckled, planets wheeled—.
But feeling *alone*'s no guarantee.
What to do with all these unsent
messages, put them in a bottle?
Plenty of empties lay around.
A page took down the pangs, line
upon line. And then? Then turned. Was gone.
At dusk, high treetops strained against
word and structure, each backlit leaf
rattling, shooting the dark rapids. . . .
And day dawned with a perfect stillness.

III

Choreography

1. Balanchine's Western Symphony

A piece, along with *Stars and Stripes,* that none
But his warmest admirers much admire,
Far from a *Symphony in Three Movements, Agon,*
Or *Four Temperaments.* Noguchi's lyre,

Which steadied the *balancés* of Orpheus,
Reborn as a banjo? Change like that shocks,
And Mr. B., his friends tell, always was
A most mysterious being—Orthodox

Romancer, genius, loon—but with an eye
On brass tacks and a hard-edged realism
That verified by dramatizing the high
Abstract, facts faced like facets of a prism.

Witness this brightly colored novelty,
Six-shooting Jacques and silky Tanaquil
Skipping through slatted swinging doors of the
(Until style touched it) mostly untouchable

Saloon, "Red River Valley," in a dude
String version, calling the folktune, *yippi-i-yo.*
File it away along with Bottom's rude
Mechanicals, with La Fontaine, Rousseau,

Modern Times, or Calder's *Circus*? Fine,
But don't complain when foregone views of art
As museum-fodder jinx what they enshrine—
Nor be surprised that Europe, for its part,

Greets simple imitation with a yawn
And saves its keenest praise for Whitman, Ives,

For Wright and Stein, John Ford and Ellington,
Offhand mythologizers of our lives. . . .

Then add one Georgian-American, no stiff
Headwinds to brave, just briefings called downstairs:
"First comes the sweat, then comes the beauty—*if*
you're very lucky and have said your prayers."

2. Mikhail Baryshnikov Dances Three Preludes *for Mark Morris*

Numberless bygone energies conspire
        in any new invention: jazz
barreled up from the Delta to New York,
        one proof of the event, Gershwin's *Preludes*.
No surprise if a star of classical

ballet extends what he can do by adding
        some steam from dance innovator
Morris, the result that here he is live
        in a black jumpsuit, white gloves,
spats, and a Cub Scout haircut,

ready to jump-start this capriccio.
        Tender, quick, precise as a squirrel—
no trembling, though, at the pauses,
        instead, an explosive freeze
fired into the next turn, the next

and the next, arms up, whirling, the gloves
        leaving a white smear in the air,
so our dazzled time-lapse take of it—
        action!—looks like Jackson Pollock, the movie,
its soundtrack dealt a downbeat from tap.

Spats whizz forward and seesaw back on
        the jump, his head popped to one side
as up go the gloves, wrists inward,
        into high flamenco attitude, then wide,
while he rickracks stage front in a blue

skip, and there must, there *must* be a rope.
        Never has gravity been so

laissez-faire when his left leg flings
        back and around, upheld by a taut
glute, and flips him aloft in the turn.

Next, bend at the waist, arms in a half-
        nelson and meet a rising spat, kick off
left, right, left again, flex to the floor,
        and bang half a yard into the
air, Fred Astaire on springs—it's a deuce

coupe now and forever, assuming
        Plato and Satchmo had it down
about ideal form and cut time, *one*
        two, New Orleans, New York, George, Mark
Russia, Mischa, this was an event.

After Neruda

His clothes stripped off the fisherman raises his spear
stalking the trapped fish that circles a rock pool
Sea   air   and man all stand motionless
Compassion like a rose maybe blossoms
at the water's edge and slowly rises
soothing the jagged moment with calm
One by one each minute seems to close
on its elder like folds in a fan
Then the naked fisherman's heart
appeased its pounding in the sea
and when the rocks were not watching
and while the wave unraveled its strength
straight to the core of that speechless world
he let fire a lightning bolt
against the still life of the stone
The spear plunged into brute matter
The struck fish throbbed rising to light
cruel flag on an impassive sea
butterfly of blood-streaked salt

A Conch from Sicily

The
Attic once
My nursery is like
An early language no longer
Spoken, a babble too small ever
Again to house adults. Yet the spiral
Stair remains, Maestro Fibonacci the builder,
Who made it pirouette downward like a clockwork
Calla. In the Southern Hemisphere it would run
Counterclockwise, yet I as well as the conchs
Down under have a silhouette like South
America, and we all smooth the path
That clothes our foot with orange
Coral enamel paneling and floor,
As far down as this loosely
Furled calyx, one concave
Rondo's calm finale—or,
If not the last, then
The next-to-last
Summing up, a
Single word:
Il tempo—
Weather,
Speed,
Time.

A Poem Named "Bashō in the Genju Hut"

A human life is measured
in a linked sequence of dwellings.
The Bashō Hut gave Bashō
both shelter and a name—
and still he burned to travel.

Genju (the monk whose name
translates as "Unreal") had died,
yet he left behind a hut
where, much later, Bashō stayed,
enacting Genju's meaning:
The world and those that dwell
under its roof are . . . *unreal.*

Call it a hut, a name
passed on from hand to hand.
His poems sheltered Bashō,
and poems translate the world:
Bashō in the Unreal Hut.

Two Greek Subjects

1. Sapphics at a Trot

Horses aren't always averse to bridles,
Yet the best is seldom a lowly numbskull.
Take it out today for a canter and you'll
Feel the resistance.

Sappho cinched strong lines to her icy darlings,
Who, alas, seemed not to appreciate them.
No, the fact remains that a cozy love life's
Not very likely—

When, that is, you choose to become a poet.
Eager, are you, ready to jump? Terrif, but
Tunes to hoof it by are a nightmare if your
Meter is awkward.

Music, is that you with a score to guide us?
Tender overtures can appease resentment.
Beauty owes a ride to the groom allaying
Stress with a rhythm.

2. *To Hermes*

Lord Quicksilver, god of erections, come down
in your winged Nikes, your hard hat brilliant
as an oiled mirror, and lend some assistance.
I have a young partner, handsome and eager,
whose love I want, whose pleasure pleases me.
When a smile as mischievous as his seems to ask
for a second round or a third, naturally
every spurred nerve aches to pump up the tempo,
like a dark horse the last heat of the day,
sweatsoaked and burning to win. My age, though,
men are long past the satyrs we once were,
flesh quickens or not after its own will or whim.
Now, I have no use for clever devices; so take
your wand (its twin snakes intertwined like vines),
touch my equipment, and work your famous magic.
If you do this, I will free two doves in your name
to fly beside you on your early morning errands.
Divine messenger boy, send me like a letter,
a fox to its burrow, a hand in its silk-lined glove.
Let me keep unwavering purpose—to embody feeling
till all the senses answer, blazing the path to our own
Olympus, no medal like the light in each other's eye.

The Alfama

How not to be destroyed by an earthquake:
we might as well absorb that lesson, too,
on foot, naturalizing one more city
(Gothic façade, orange vendor, bumpy cobbles)
to memory, as we negotiate
the ups and askew downs of a district
that says, "Build on rock and build in stone.
I did, and survived 1755."

Former Moorish fort in golden limestone,
Castelo São Jorge, high up among swaying
cypresses, took the extra precaution
of abandoning its military role to become
a park, complete with albino peacock
and volunteer musician playing Sousa tunes
on alto recorder. Then a shift
to Ravel, something reflective
for strollers picking their way
among lucid puddles of fresh rainwater
as they circle the ramparts,
where a soldier on leave
flashes his medals at two French schoolgirls.

                        Several levels lower,
perpetuity was never in doubt
for vertical tenements crowding
a street plan too tortuous to provide
space for something more palatial.
Poverty's dependable, it's always
with us. . . . The grandmother in black
propped on an elbow in her ground-floor window
has kept her vigil there time out of mind,
just like that age-old canary spinning

vocal ornament in the gloom behind her,
who, unaware of evolution in music,
broadcasts the same song that Vasco and Camões knew.
Safe from disaster and from change,
it's never even learned to sing *fado.*

*   *

Farther on, the guidebook's two-star vista:
one side flanked by housing, a downscale
minipark offers for comparison
cubist perspectives on the lower town,

with, meanwhile, their duplicate in a mural
of sea-blue *azulejos.* (Perhaps because
tiles impose a grid on what they show,
a people conditioned by them didn't fail

to equip its navigators with a map
of the known cosmos ruled in latitude
and longitude—the most decisive, one
partitioning the Indies between co-claimant

Iberian crowns.) From here Alfama tenants
could wistfully applaud as sails blazoned
with blood-red crosses billowed up the Tagus,
past the Torre de Belém, brimful with gold.

But not for them. Gold built fine palaces,
it raised up walls, commissioned ornaments,
planted interior gardens—most of which
found destruction when the earthquake struck.

A Marriage in the Nineties

They've said the art of poetry resembles,
on one hand, song, with poet as the rara
avis that makes his birdcage play in tune;
it's also been compared to hard labor.

Scrubbing our kitchen tiles today, on all
fours, and humming something like the blues,
I thought of Yeats's line from "Adam's Curse,"
Better go down upon your marrow-bones,

and so forth. How much did a man with servants
know about it? As the decals say,
"I'd rather be writing." But Manhattanites
like us don't keep a car, so where to stick it?

Don't answer that. (Polish, polish, polish.)
It's not that you don't do your share, Chris;
you're a good "husband," women's lib won't help.
Wages of poetry got us at least this far:

we've all of three small rooms to keep in shape.
Just maybe two of these sixth-floor apartments
are decent-sized, and only one tenant straight—
a youngish, ash-blond broker from Belgium,

who that first spring after arriving took
the measure of his present situation
and planted redwood terrace-garden boxes
with pansies by the hundreds, nothing but pansies!

I watched him crouch over small purple-and-yellow
Pekingese faces and waved when he looked up.
Life in the Village. He and a series of girlfriends
haven't seemed flustered at all, they've been nice neighbors.

A marriage in the Nineties. New York City,
if we sign papers, will consider us
"domestic partners." Somehow, though, it feels
more romantic not to. Getting older

pushes mavericks always further toward
the middle class, so why speed up the process?
Insurance offers safety but soaks up feeling—
which brings in risk. Remember Portugal,

the anger we routinely felt for whatever
addict or refugee it was that nicked
our luggage from the car? Those Avis decals
tipped them off, most likely. Property

is theft, granted, but theft of property
also felt like theft. My diary gone,
snapshots we'd taken, worthless to *them,* as well
as other items of "sentimental value."

Both sets of house keys, too, which meant having
a locksmith break into our own apartment
(Russian, moonlighting, his real profession
reproducing Baroque violins).

He scratched his beard and squinted like a watch
repairman at locks he then hauled off and smashed.
At least we got a smile and compassionate handshake,
plus new keys and a bill for two hundred bucks.

Disaster? No, nothing like what happened
to Christophe (our Belgian) the same starcrossed,
snowbound day we returned, his bedroom flooded
by a heating pipe that froze, then cracked, then spewed.

Or to our next-door neighbor Steve, just out
of intensive care for a bout with pneumocystis
during his vacation in Key West,
two balmy weeks with an I.V. in his arm. . . .

We're very lucky. No microbes have broken
in and made off with our lives or health.
Nor are we homeless like Devane, the guy
who sits all day outside our building, hailing

strangers or neighbors like us who halfway know him.
Time and again I've said, "Devane, a man
as smart as you has no business on the street."
He agrees, yeah-yeah, and blames cocaine and booze,

which he plans to kick someday. Today?
Well, no, it helps him stand the cold and damp,
but one great morning . . . ! He also tells me he's
bisexual, but that one I let pass.

As a schoolboy in, say, Brussels, Christophe—
funny, it just occurs to me that you
and he have the same name—may well have read
Pascal's *Pensées,* as I did back in college.

He'd probably recognize the one that says,
"The more intelligence one has the more
people one finds original. Commonplace
people see no difference between men."

Devane, for instance, calculating each
potential donor's quirks and soft spots so
he can "articulate sweet sounds together,"
magic words to make it rain down gold

or silver, any tribute but the pennies
he loathes but must of course pretend to want.
Or Steve next door, who says he prayed to survive
once more because he hadn't yet determined

his true identity and what he's here for.
Or us, sweetheart, this February 14th,
which I didn't think of in time to find
a present. Middle age's curse, defective

memory—as good an excuse as any
"for getting it all down." That, and a chance
to image feeling with exactitude,
love for an irreplaceable hunk, whatever.

From Lisbon to Beijing to Brussels, song
breaks forth to say inclinations have changed:
"The life devoid of sentiment is not
worth living," a news flash ricocheted off Telstar,

dense wavelength webwork of the global village
where we make a present of ourselves
to stranger and neighbor, hoping it's the thought
that counts. Come this June, I'll write mine out

and see if Christophe wants to anthologize
one more *pensée* with those in his terrace boxes.
To you, Chris, hearts and flowers of the day,
and kitchen tiles that will just have to do.

Water Like a Philosopher's Stone

Now, out of skies like lead, as the hoary old
cliché describes them, comes a massive snowfall,
no doubt the one barometers deep in the bone
and wide-eyed weathercasters were predicting.

An unplanned celebration for us all:
errands done, there's time, before we scuttle
home, for a twilight walk, as fine-grained drifts
of industrial diamond renovate a city.

Transmutation of the commonplace,
is it, straightforwardness as magic, making
those thrown-out, ugly-duckling shopping bags
turn sculptural, like snow-white swans at gaze?

Or cannily revealing zinc-gray chain-link
playground fences as the crochet network
they are; that streetlamp, a North Sea lighthouse,
which now comes on and paves the street with gold—
with light. It's still *our* street, and, as such, home.

Insertion Arias

Entering a cave, or stepping outside at night,
artificial blindness, temporary
but absolute. And if I lost my sight,
the long-distance sense, the avenue to color,
would speech and music be enough to live on?
No more sunsets filtered through palm branches,
no plunge of snowflakes into the breakers,
no more mountains overhung with a crush of stars;
no rose window, no Yoruba head, no pietà
no more meeting your eyes filling up with light.

Stretched out side by side, catching our breath again,
we've listened, while heartbeats subside
and fresh sweat dries, to a solo voice, this
composer or that, Mozart most often, one of his
"insertion arias," say, *Vorrei spiegarvi, oh Dio,*
which was folded into (because a soprano
demanded something with more fire, more muscle)
an otherwise defunct opera by Anfossi.

Eyes closed, we let intentional sound sink in.
For a while, all we are is a voice
as it steps and glides over textured strings
made one harmonic flesh with woodwinds.
The music's pulse is hard to tell from ours,
and blind attention doubles what it hears.
Dancelike themes and pitched words
in an old language not by me always
translatable replace the "I love you"
we save for times we mean it to the bone.

Love itself's one of the threats to love,
like the stimulus sustained so long it dims
or goes inaudible. To offer more

than a wide-eyed, unreflective stare,
simple tact at last reverses the scope,
turns inward and finds another you, cocooned
in second nature like a future swallowtail,
safe from judge, senator, or cardinal,
whoever might try to forbid what we feel.

Obstacles, threats, and blights all over,
yet if involuntary hope scores its goal,
then you'll be present, tall, warm, steady,
from now on—though you'll also day by day
go off to work, managing on your own;
and then come back, most months before nightfall,
a reunion intenser for the separation.

Years mount up, and I have fifteen more
than you. For the optimum scenario,
a hand-in-hand walk toward embers of a sunset,
likelihood provides no support at all.
Would you accept the proposition
that death puts an end to seeing,
but not to *hearing*, those we've lost?
(The voice per se, maybe not, but at least
its musical equivalent—a motion, a heartbeat
at the core of things, a penetrating insound.)

This is you beside me now, and the distance
is close or far as we make it.
Few singers try to manage without
accompaniment, the fulfillment of an outcry—
even if what was meant is never fully explained.
There: the aria's done, translation I hope
provided for; and now I can breathe again.

NOTES

Many of the following notes will strike some readers as superfluous and are added merely as a time-saving convenience for those uncertain about particular references in some of the poems.

"Stepson Elegy"

The Cumaean Sibyl is the oracle Aeneas visits in Book Six of *Aeneid*. Their encounter is found beginning at line 42. During their conversation Aeneas promises to raise a shrine to Phoebus (Apollo) and to Trivia, an aspect of the moon-and-fertility goddess Hecate, whose home is in the Underworld and who is concerned with crossroads (cf. Latin *trivia*, "a crossroads"). The Sibyl conducts Aeneas to the Underworld, where he receives confirmation of his Italian mission. "Il Mantovano" : "the Mantuan," or Virgil, who was born near Mantua in what is now Lombardy. In the *Commedia*, Dante often calls Virgil "il Mantovano."

"Lago di Como: *The Cypresses*"

On the shores of Lake Como in Italy a species of cypress originally from Portugal (Latin name, *Lusitania*) are found in abundance. Olive trees, first brought by Greek immigrants, flourish there as well. The Lisbon earthquake occurred in 1755.

"The Dead Sea"

The basin, several hundred feet below sea level, into which the Jordan River empties, with no further outlet. On its northwestern shore, the caves of Qumran have become a place of pilgrimage because they were the dwellings of the scribes who produced the texts known as the Dead Sea Scrolls. "Black fire on white fire" is a term used by the medieval cabalists to describe the Torah.

"Jaffa"

The modern city dates from an ancient one known in the Bible as Joppa. Accounts of the Andromeda legend locate her father Cepheus's kingdom in Joppa. The period of the British Mandate (or temporary colonial administration) in Palestine began in 1923 after the 1917 Balfour Declaration, in which Britain undertook to establish a national homeland for the Jews in Palestine, but the terms of the proclamation were not fulfilled until 1948. "Tel Jaffa" in Arabic means "the hill of Jaffa."

"Caesarea"

A Roman city on the Mediterranean shore, whose present-day ruins include an amphitheater. Acanthus is a wild plant the form of whose leaves is incorporated in the design of the Corinthian capital. Actors in classical theater used *personae* (masks) and buskins (elevated shoes) as theatrical aids. A trireme was a Roman ship using three ranks of galley slaves as rowers.

"In Safed"

Safed is a small town in northern Galilee that, after the expulsion of the Spanish Jews in 1492, became a center for several scholars and cabalists, including Moses Cordovero, Isaac Luria, and Joseph Karo. Karo is renowned as the author of the Shulan Arukh, a commentary on rabbinic practice. The *Shekhinah* is the presence or immanence of God in the created world. Beliefs around this concept developed in medieval Judaism, which, partly because the word has feminine gender, attributed feminine nature to this manifestation of deity. Joseph Karo said he found Shekhinah in the Mishnah Torah. (Later proponents of this doctrine have asserted it can be found as well in the Foundation Wall of the Second Temple in Jerusalem.) Divine Presence was also celebrated in an annual spring rite when adepts dressed in white robes and went down to the fields below Safed to salute Her.

"Musical Sacrifice"

Verse sections of this sequence have been assigned names of various musical forms, most of them familiar, though perhaps not *Sprechstimme*, which means a kind of chantlike singing close to the sound of the spoken voice. Schönberg uses it in his song cycle *Pierrot Lunaire. Die Verwandlung* is the German title of the Kafka novella known in English as *The Metamorphosis*, though the word also means "transfiguration" and "scene change" (as in theater). In Czech, *kavka* means "jackdaw," or, more simply, "crow." Section 13 incorporates several statements that Kafka made into a text otherwise invented. The "Holy of Holies" refers to a room at the center of the

Second Temple in Jerusalem (in Hebrew, *debir*), which no one except the High Priest was allowed to enter, and he only once during the year. Except for a low stone platform, the room contained nothing—or rather, pure, sacred space.

"Michel Gérard's Observatory"

Marina Temkina, who immigrated to the United States in 1970, has published two collections of poetry in Russian with Syntaxis Press. Michel Gérard, a French sculptor now living in New York with Ms. Temkina, is the person addressed in the poem.

"*Balanchine's* Western Symphony"

The ballet choreographer George Balanchine was born in Georgia, subject to the Russian Empire before the Revolution. For the New York City Ballet he choreographed more than a hundred ballets, including *Western Symphony* (to music by Hershey Kay) and those titles mentioned in this poem's opening lines. One of the props used in his *Orpheus* (designed by Isamu Noguchi) was a stylized lyre. Tanaquil Leclercq and Jacques d'Amboise were among the first performers of *Western Symphony*. The last two lines are quoted from Balanchine.

"*Mikhail Baryshnikov Dances* Three Preludes *for Mark Morris*"

The Russian dancer Mikhail (Mischa) Baryshnikov, after a brilliant career in classical ballet, has performed in many modern dance works, including the recent *Three Preludes,* choreographed by Mark Morris to music by George Gershwin.

"A Poem Named 'Bashō in the Genju Hut'"

The Japanese poet Bashō (1644–94), born in the city of Ueno, is probably the greatest practitioner of haiku as well as the *haibun,* or poetic diary. His real name was Matsuo Munefusa, but in the spring of his thirty-sixth year a disciple planted a plantain or banana tree next to the hut near Edo (modern Tokyo) where the poet was living. The Japanese for "banana" is "bashō," and soon the poet's disciples began calling the hut the "Bashō Hut," and its inhabitant "the Master of the Bashō Hut." The poet was fond of the tree and accepted the new epithet as his own name.

In 1690 he spent some time near Lake Biwa, staying in a hut where a Buddhist monk had once lived. The monk's Buddhist name was Genju, or "Unreal," and the hut inherited the name of its resident. About his stay there Bashō wrote one of his best-known works, the *haibun* titled "An Essay on the Unreal Dwelling," which takes up the Buddhist themes of the illusory and transitory nature of human life.

"Sapphics at a Trot"

Sapphic meter in Greek and Latin poetry is based on syllable length, not syllable stress. A number of poets writing sapphics in English have simply substituted stress for length in the metric template. A few have attempted to use length alone, but ears conditioned by English accentuation don't perceive any regular pattern in these experiments. Here I have worked to make syllable length and stress coincide, where, as in Greek, a long syllable is defined as one having a long vowel or diphthong, or any vowel followed by more than one consonant.

"The Alfama"

The Alfama is the oldest quarter of Lisbon, dating back to Phoenician times. For many centuries it has been a working-class district. Built on a foundation of rock, it was not much damaged by the earthquake of 1755. *Azulejos* are ceramic tiles, a Portuguese specialty, sometimes used in tableaux like the one described in this poem, with individual tiles cooperating in a gridded mosaic to depict landscapes, townscapes, or portraits. In 1494 the Treaty of Tordesillas established a longitude in the Western Hemisphere, east of which all newly discovered lands were assigned to Portugal, and west of which to Spain.

Special gratitude is due to the Rockefeller Foundation for a month's residency
at the Bellagio Conference Center in 1992, and to the MacDowell Colony
and its staff for a month's residency in 1994.

The author wishes to thank the following periodicals where poems first appeared,
sometimes in different form:

Agni: "Stepson Elegy"
Blue Moon Review: "Michel Gérard's Observatory"
The Boston Review: "Maui: Concerto for Island and Developer"
The Kenyon Review: "Sugar Cane"; "To Hermes"
The Nation: "Caesarea"; "Parallels"; "The Shouters"; "Wonderbread"
The New Republic: "Balanchine's *Western Symphony*"; "The Cloak of Invisibility";
    "*Lago di Como:* The Cypresses"
The New England Review: "Jaffa"; "The Unknown Poets"
The New Yorker: "A Marriage in the Nineties"
The Paris Review: "Insertion Arias"; "Philosophy"
Partisan Review: "Water Like a Philosopher's Stone"
Pequod: "A Goya Reproduction" (under the title "Goya's Don Manuel Osorio
    Manrique de Zuñiga")
Ploughshares: "Musical Sacrifice"
Princeton University Library Chronicle: "Sapphics at a Trot"
Raritan: "The Bonfire"
Salmagundi: "The Alfama"; "Mikhail Baryshnikov Dances *Three Preludes* for
    Mark Morris"
Slate: "A Poem Named 'Bashō in the Genju Hut'"
Verse: "After Neruda"
Western Humanities Review: "A Conch from Sicily"; "Little Erie Railroad"